Georgia, My State
Rivers

Ocmulgee River

by Amelia J. Pohl

STATE STANDARDS PUBLISHING LLC ®

Your State • Your Standards • Your Grade Level

Dear Educators, Librarians and Parents . . .

Thank you for choosing the *"Georgia, My State"* Series! We have designed this series to support the Georgia Department of Education's Georgia Performance Standards for elementary level Georgia studies. Each book in the series has been written at appropriate grade level as measured by the ATOS Readability Formula for Books (Accelerated Reader), the Lexile Framework for Reading, and the Fountas & Pinnell Benchmark Assessment System for Guided Reading. Photographs and/or illustrations, captions, and other design elements have been included to provide supportive visual messaging to enhance text comprehension. Glossary and Word Index sections introduce key new words and help young readers develop skills in locating and combining information.

We wish you all success in using the *"Georgia, My State"* Series to meet your student or child's learning needs. For additional sources of information, see www.georgiaencyclopedia.org.

Jill Ward, President

Publisher
State Standards Publishing, LLC
1788 Quail Hollow
Hamilton, GA 31811
USA
1.866.740.3056
www.statestandardspublishing.com

Library of Congress Cataloging-in-Publication Data
Pohl, Amelia J., 1984-
   Ocmulgee River / by Amelia J. Pohl.
      p. cm. -- (Georgia, my state. Rivers)
   Includes index.
   ISBN-13: 978-1-935077-56-5 (hardcover)
   ISBN-10: 1-935077-56-2 (hardcover)
   ISBN-13: 978-1-935077-63-3 (pbk.)
   ISBN-10: 1-935077-63-5 (pbk.)
   1. Ocmulgee River (Ga.)--Description and travel--Juvenile literature. I. Title.
   F292.O27P64 2009
   917.58'50444--dc22
                                      2009036092

Printed in the United States of America, North Mankato, Minnesota, October 2009, 070209.

About the Author

Amelia Pohl is a graduate of the University of Georgia's noted Grady College of Journalism and Mass Communication, one of the oldest and most distinguished communication programs in the country. She is a graduate of the Grady at Oxford, England, program of study and is a member of the National Scholars Honor Society. She lives in Athens, Georgia.

Table of Contents

Appalachian Plateau

Blue Ridge Mountains

Valley and Ridge

Piedmont

Oconee River

Ocmulgee River

Altamaha River

Upper Coastal Plain

Lower Coastal Plain

MY STATE

The Ocmulgee River is in central Georgia.

Let's Explore!

Hi, I'm Bagster! Let's explore the Ocmulgee River! It is located in central Georgia. This is the middle part of Georgia. The Ocmulgee River and the Oconee River are tributaries of the Altamaha River. A **tributary** is a stream that flows into another stream or other body of water.

Appalachian Plateau

Blue Ridge Mountains

Valley and Ridge

Piedmont

Yellow River

Alcovy River

South River

Jackson Lake

Ocmulgee River

Upper Coastal Plain

Lower Coastal Plain

The Ocmulgee cuts a narrow channel like this one through the red clay soil.

A Narrow Channel

The **headwaters** of the Ocmulgee are the South River, Yellow River, and Alcovy River. They join in Jackson Lake. This is where the river starts. The Ocmulgee cuts a narrow **channel** through the red clay soil. This is the river's path. The river bank is very tall in some places! The water often looks muddy.

Appalachian Plateau

Blue
Ridge
Mountains

Valley
and
Ridge

Piedmont

Lake →
Juliette

Ocmulgee River

Upper Coastal Plain

Lower Coastal Plain

Lake Juliette

Water from the Ocmulgee is pumped to Lake Juliette. It helps make electricity.

Pumping Water from the River

Further south, water is pumped from the river. It goes to Lake Juliette. The water is turned into steam. It helps make electricity. There are **rapids**

in this part of the Ocmulgee. The water flows fast!

There are rapids in this part of the Ocmulgee River.

Appalachian Plateau

Blue
Ridge
Mountains

Valley
and
Ridge

Piedmont

Macon ★

Ocmulgee River

Upper Coastal Plain

Lower Coastal Plain

Water is pumped into a reservoir at Macon.

Water for Macon

The Ocmulgee flows to Macon. Water is pumped out of the river again. It goes into a **reservoir**. A reservoir is a lake that provides drinking water. The city also puts **wastewater** back in the river. This is water that has been used in homes and businesses. It is cleaned before going back into the river.

The Ocmulgee flows to Macon.

Appalachian Plateau

Blue Ridge Mountains

Valley and Ridge

Piedmont

Macon

Ocmulgee River

Fall Line

Upper Coastal Plain

Lower Coastal Plain

The Ocmulgee Mounds are over 1,000 years old!

Ancient Indian Mounds!

The river tumbles over the **fall line**. This is an area of land that falls steeply. It passes the Ocmulgee National Monument. Ancient **Indian mounds** are here. They are over 1,000 years old! The mounds were temples and meeting places. Indians also buried their chiefs in the mounds.

It's a long way to the top!

Walnut Creek is a wetland.

Bond Swamp is a wetland.

Black bears live in Bond Swamp!

Wetlands and Bears!

There are **wetlands** around the Ocmulgee. A wetland is land that is covered in water all or some of the time. Walnut Creek is a wetland. Cutgrass grows here. Watch out! Its blades are sharp! Bond Swamp is also a wetland. Hardwood trees grow in the water. Black bears live here, too!

Sandbars build up around the river.

Silt Makes Sandbars

The Ocmulgee crosses into the Coastal Plain. The land is flat here. The water slows and becomes more shallow. The river gets wider. There is **silt** in the water here. Silt is soft sand that floats in the water or falls to the bottom. **Sandbars** build up around the river. These are like sand beaches.

Spanish moss hangs
from the trees.

People fish for catfish and bass.

Appalachian Plateau

Blue
Ridge
Mountains

Valley
and
Ridge

Piedmont

Macon ★

Warner Robins ★

Hawkinsville ★

Ocmulgee River

Upper Coastal Plain

Lower Coastal Plain

A Place to Paddle and Fish

The Ocmulgee flows through Warner Robins and Hawkinsville. Spanish moss hangs in the trees along the river. Many people paddle canoes down the river. People also fish for catfish and bass.

People paddle canoes down the river.

The Ocmulgee and the Oconee make the Altamaha.

Oconee River

Ocmulgee River

Altamaha River

Appalachian Plateau

Blue Ridge Mountains

Valley and Ridge

Piedmont

Oconee River

Ocmulgee River

Macon

Warner Robins

Hawkinsville

Lumber City

Big Bend

Altamaha River

Upper Coastal Plain

Lower Coastal Plain

MY STATE

The Ocmulgee is a peaceful river and an important tributary.

An Important Tributary

The Ocmulgee River turns east. This is called the Big Bend. There is not much **development** here. People have not built homes and businesses. It flows to Lumber City. Then it joins the Oconee River. Together, the two rivers form the Altamaha River. The Ocmulgee River ends here. It is a peaceful river and an important tributary.

Glossary

channel – The path of a river.

development – Building homes and businesses in areas that were natural.

fall line – An area of land that falls steeply.

headwaters – The place where a river starts.

Indian mounds – Places that Indians used as temples or meeting places. They also buried their chiefs in mounds.

rapids – Water in a river that flows fast.

reservoir – A lake that provides drinking water.

sandbars – Mounds of sand that build up around rivers.

silt – Soft sand that floats in the water or falls to the bottom.

tributary – A stream that flows into another stream or other body of water.

wastewater – Water that has been used in homes and businesses.

wetlands – Places that are covered in water all or some of the time.

Word Index

Image Credits

p. 4   Ocmulgee: © Alan Cressler, Flickr.com
p. 6   Channel: Photo courtesy of Georgia Department of Economic Development
p. 8   Power plant: Photo courtesy of Antennas, Wikipedia.com
p. 9   Rapids: © Alan Cressler, Flickr.com
p. 10 Reservoir: © Mark Strozier, iStockphoto.com; Macon: Photo courtesy of Georgia Department of Economic Development
p. 12 Mounds: Photos courtesy of Georgia Department of Economic Development
p. 14 Bear: © Outdoorsman, fotolia.com; Creek: © Alan Cressler, Flickr.com; Swamp: © Diane Carr, Columbus, Georgia
p. 16 Sandbar: © Alan Cressler, Flickr.com
p. 18 Fishermen: Photo courtesy of Georgia Department of Economic Development; Spanish moss: © Jonathan Lyons, iStockphoto.com
p. 19 Canoeists: Photo courtesy of Georgia Department of Economic Development
p. 20 Ocmulgee River: © Alan Cressler, Flickr.com; Rivers Aerial: Courtesy of the Altamaha Riverkeeper

Georgia, My State Rivers

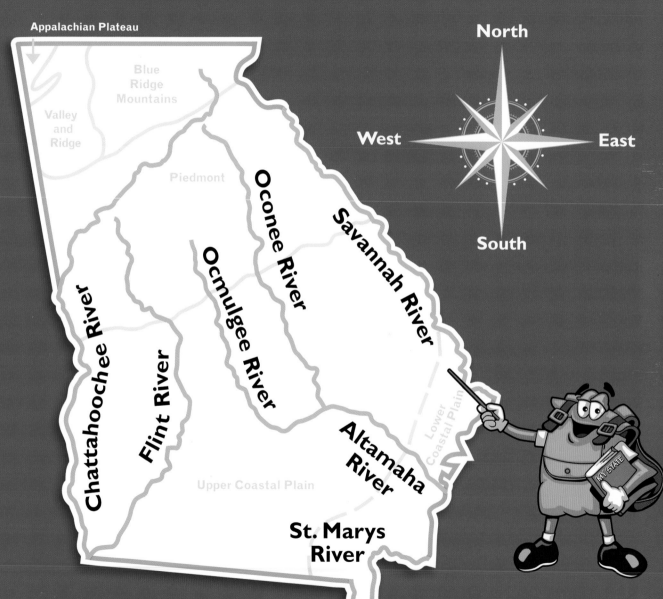

Appalachian Plateau

Blue Ridge Mountains

Valley and Ridge

Piedmont

North

West

East

South

Oconee River

Savannah River

Ocmulgee River

Chattahoochee River

Flint River

Altamaha River

Lower Coastal Plain

Upper Coastal Plain

St. Marys River

MY STATE